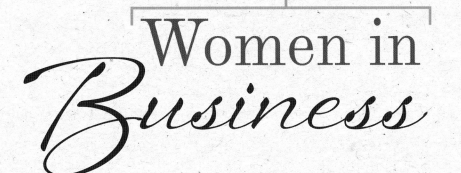

Women in
Business

BY ALEXIS BURLING

CONTENT CONSULTANT
Diana M. Hechavarria, PhD
Professor, Center for Entrepreneurship
University of South Florida

Essential Library

An Imprint of Abdo Publishing | abdopublishing.com

002000544570

WOMEN'S LIVES *in* *History*

abdopublishing.com

Published by Abdo Publishing, a division of ABDO, PO Box 398166, Minneapolis, Minnesota 55439. Copyright © 2017 by Abdo Consulting Group, Inc. International copyrights reserved in all countries. No part of this book may be reproduced in any form without written permission from the publisher. Essential Library™ is a trademark and logo of Abdo Publishing.

Printed in the United States of America, North Mankato, Minnesota
052016
092016

THIS BOOK CONTAINS
RECYCLED MATERIALS

Cover Photo: Shutterstock Images
Interior Photos: Eugene Gologursky/WireImage/Getty Images, 4–5; Gabe Ginsberg/ESSENCE/Getty Images, 8; Bebeto Matthews/AP Images, 10–11; The New York Public Library, 14–15, 20–21; Library of Congress, 16–17; Science Source, 19; Alan Fisher/Library of Congress, 22; Marjory Collins/Library of Congress, 24; American Press Association/Library of Congress, 26–27; Everett Historical/Shutterstock Images, 30, 34–35; Everett Collection/Newscom, 32, 37; Hulton Archive/Getty Images, 38; Bill Sauro/Library of Congress, 40; Richard Harbus/AP Images, 43; Piero Oliosi/Polaris/Newscom, 44; Frank C. Curtin/AP Images, 46–47; Rex Features/AP Images, 48; David Fowler/Shutterstock Images, 50; Ewing Galloway\UIG\Everett Collection, 52–53; UPI/Newscom, 56; AP Images, 57 (top), 57 (bottom); Harvey Georges/AP Images, 58–59; Everett Collection/Shutterstock Images, 61; Shutterstock Images, 63, 88, 89; March Marcho/Shutterstock Images, 65; Lynn Goldsmith/Corbis, 66–67, 86–87; Helga Esteb/Shutterstock Images, 69; Evan Agostini/AP Images, 71; Larry Busacca/WireImage for Jones New York/Getty Images, 73; Deposit Photos/Glow Images, 74–75; Eric Risberg/AP Images, 77; Tim Wagner/ZumaPress/Newscom, 78–79; Christopher Halloran/Shutterstock Images, 81; Mario Tama/Getty Images News/Thinkstock, 82; Jean-Christophe Bott/EPA/Newscom, 84–85; Marla Aufmuth/Texas Conference for Women/Getty Images, 90; Jeff Chiu/AP Images, 92–93; Clint Spaulding/PatrickMcMullan.com/AP Images, 95; Alberto Martinez/Austin American-Statesman/PSG/Newscom, 96–97

Editor: Mirella Miller
Series Designer: Maggie Villaume

Cataloging-in-Publication Data
Names: Burling, Alexis, author.
Title: Women in business / by Alexis Burling.
Description: Minneapolis, MN : Abdo Publishing, [2017] | Series: Women's lives
    in history | Includes bibliographical references and index.
Identifiers: LCCN 2015960341 | ISBN 9781680782905 (lib. bdg.) |
    ISBN 9781680774849 (ebook)
Subjects: LCSH: Businesswomen--Juvenile literature. | Women executives--
    --Juvenile literature. | Entrepreneurship--Juvenile literature. | Women in the
    professions--Juvenile literature.
Classification: DDC 330--dc23
LC record available at http://lccn.loc.gov/2015960341

Contents

Kimberly Bryant's nonprofit caught Winfrey's attention, earning Bryant grant money to grow her organization.

CHAPTER ONE

Kimberly Bryant: Champion of Change

On November 15, 2014, the crowd in the packed arena in San Jose, California, was charged with energy. It was Oprah Winfrey's last stop during her whirlwind eight-city tour for her one-woman show. The media mogul and self-help guru was about to announce who would receive the eighth and final Standing O-Vation award—a $25,000 grant given to an extraordinary "life trailblazer."[1] The audience of more than 10,000 people was eagerly waiting to see who the lucky winner would be.[2]

In each city on Winfrey's tour, a Standing O-Vation was awarded to a woman working to change the world for the better while motivating others to make positive changes in their own lives and communities. "[This time, we've] chosen a bold woman from San Francisco," said Winfrey, looking out at the crowd. "Where is Kimberly Bryant? Kimberly Bryant, come on up here!"[3]

The stadium erupted in applause. With tears in her eyes, Bryant—the founder of Black Girls CODE, a nonprofit organization dedicated to introducing girls of color, ages 7 to 17, to the field of technology and computer science—walked onto the stage. A biographical video detailing some of her major accomplishments played on a large screen behind her as she proudly accepted the award. When the presentation was over, Winfrey clasped Bryant's hand, and, together, the two women lifted their joined arms above their heads in triumph.

Tough Beginnings

Before founding Black Girls CODE, Bryant had worked in the biotechnology industry for more than 20 years as a software engineer at top pharmaceutical companies such as Merck and Pfizer. But her path to success was not easy. As an adolescent, Bryant did not have access to a computer at home, nor was she exposed to any technology-related classes in high school. Her first experience with Fortran, a computer programming language, was not until her freshman year in college at Vanderbilt University in Nashville, Tennessee, in 1985.

Yet despite her late introduction to the world of computer programming, Bryant excelled in her introductory classes and wanted to learn more. Excited by the rise in popularity of personal computers and the advances being made by tech companies such as Intel and Microsoft, she decided to major in electrical engineering with a minor in computer science. Though she continued to earn top grades, her four years at Vanderbilt's School of Engineering were a struggle. As one of very few women, let alone African-American women, in her undergraduate classes, she felt like an outsider. Competition was fierce, and many of the coveted internship opportunities went to her white male colleagues, who better fit the stereotypical profile of a capable computer scientist.

After Bryant graduated, her first few years in the workforce were no less daunting. "One of the first experiences I had with being a double minority was being introduced to the rest of the staff and my team by my manager and him saying, 'Well, for Kimberly coming on, we got a twofer; she's a woman *and* she's a person of

INFLUENTIAL MENTORS

Bryant grew up in a low-income neighborhood in North Memphis, Tennessee, during the late 1960s and 1970s. She did not have many role models and spent most of her days tagging along with her older brother, playing video games with him and his friends. Bryant says she initially planned to become a lawyer. But because of excellent grades in science and math, she changed her course when applying to colleges. In an interview for *Wired* magazine, Bryant attributes the switch to two female African-American guidance counselors who were instrumental in encouraging her to pursue a career in engineering. Having those mentors and support was essential, Bryant says.

Bryant's commitment to making coding more accessible to girls of color has earned her numerous awards.

color'" Bryant recalled of this experience in a video interview with Winfrey. "You can imagine how I felt as a new engineer, being introduced to my peers as a twofer."[5]

With hard work and steadfast determination, Bryant learned to look beyond the gender bias and racial discrimination and thrived. Then, in 2010, her 12-year-old daughter attended a Stanford University summer camp geared toward teaching kids how to code, or write programming instructions for computers and apps. She was the only child of color and one of very few girls in the group. Bryant knew she needed to act. She left the corporate world, and in April 2011, she founded Black Girls CODE.

Building the Future

According to the US Bureau of Labor Statistics, 1.4 million science, technology, engineering, and math (STEM)-related jobs are expected to flood the marketplace by 2020.[6] But as of 2014, African-American women make up only 2 percent of the science and engineering workforce in the United States. This contrasts

CODE SCHOOL FEVER

When Bryant started Black Girls CODE, she was tapping into a nationwide trend, especially one targeting college graduates and professionals. In 2014 alone, nearly 6,000 people completed a coding boot camp—a crash course that provides instruction on how to build websites or apps using a computer-programming language. The course is full time—five days a week for eight hours a day—and can last anywhere from six weeks to three months. Today there are more than 80 coding schools around the country. Tuition is expensive. Some cost nearly $18,000.[7] But the rewards are potentially huge: code school graduates can often command better jobs and higher salaries.

with white men making up 51 percent and white women accounting for 18 percent in the same fields.[8] Judging by these figures, African-American women are vastly underrepresented in many tech-related careers. In Bryant's mind, it was up to her to train a new generation so they would have the skills to take a more prominent role in the growing industry.

When she launched Black Girls CODE in 2011, Bryant started small. She hired two staff members and used her own money to fund the organization until large tech companies such as Google signed on as corporate sponsors. In her first one-week summer training program in San Francisco, California, she focused on teaching girls aged 10 to 13 entry-level tools they might use in their everyday lives, such as video game and website development.

As word began to spread about Black Girls CODE and girls as young as 7 and as old as 17 expressed interest in attending future sessions, Bryant added a wider variety of classes, including robotics and complex programming languages. She also took the girls on field trips to tech companies such as Facebook and staged girls-only "hackathons"—events where students could come together to solve problems by writing apps.

By 2015, Bryant's staff had grown to five people. Today, Black Girls CODE has transformed from a local start-up into a national phenomenon. The group's volunteers number into the thousands and have trained more than 8,000 students in nine cities around the United States and in Johannesburg, South Africa.[9] Bryant hopes that by 2040 the organization will have taught one million girls of all racial and ethnic backgrounds to code.[10]

In addition to forming a valuable organization, Bryant has achieved personal milestones too. In August 2012, she was given the prestigious Jefferson Award for Community Service because of her efforts to support communities in the San Francisco Bay area. In 2013, *Business Insider* magazine named her as one of the 25 Most Influential African-Americans in Technology, and traditionally black publication *Ebony* included her on its Power 100 list. And in 2014, Bryant was given the first Women Who Rule in Technology Award by Google and the political news publication *Politico*.

Visionary Women

Bryant is one of the many women throughout recent history who have navigated uncharted territory in order to make great strides in business. There were others before her who paved the way for future generations. Madam C. J. Walker became one of the first female self-made millionaires in 1905 by creating specialized hair products for African-American hair. Margaret Rudkin cooked up a recipe for wheat bread in the late 1930s. It was so healthy and delicious that it inspired Pepperidge Farm, a bakery Rudkin founded that would blossom into a $28 million enterprise.[11]

During the second half of the 1900s and into the 2000s, women such as talk show host and spiritual guru Winfrey and Facebook COO Sheryl Sandberg continue to shape the world's progress in ways never imagined. Others, such as actress Sofía Vergara and biotech start-up founder Elizabeth Holmes, have left their mark in all areas of business, from clothing and cosmetics to medicine and technology. Each of these women faced gender biases and overcame obstacles not only in the workplace but also in society at large.

If there is a lesson to be learned in Bryant's path, it is that success takes patience, strength, and an unshakable vision for a brighter future. "Initially, I just wanted to take money out of my savings and send a group of girls to the same summer camp so my daughter wouldn't be alone," Bryant said. "But now [Black Girls CODE] is in nine cities. . . . That's a lot of little black and brown girls learning to code, and I just know that many of our students are going to go on to become leaders in technology. I have absolutely no doubt."[12]

A LEADER IN PHILANTHROPY

When Melinda French started dating her boss, Bill Gates, at Microsoft in 1987, the first thing she noticed was his busy schedule. But when he proposed six years later and the two married in 1994, little did she know that she, too, was about to get much busier. That same year, the couple started the William H. Gates Foundation, with Melinda as cochair and in charge of the day-to-day planning of much of the philanthropic programs.

For more than 20 years, Gates's efforts and donations have improved the lives of thousands of people in need across the world. One of the foundation's main focuses is its Global Health Program. The initiative partners with organizations around the world to develop effective and affordable vaccines and medicines for communities in need. In 2012, Gates pledged $560 million toward helping women in third-world countries gain access to contraceptives.[13]

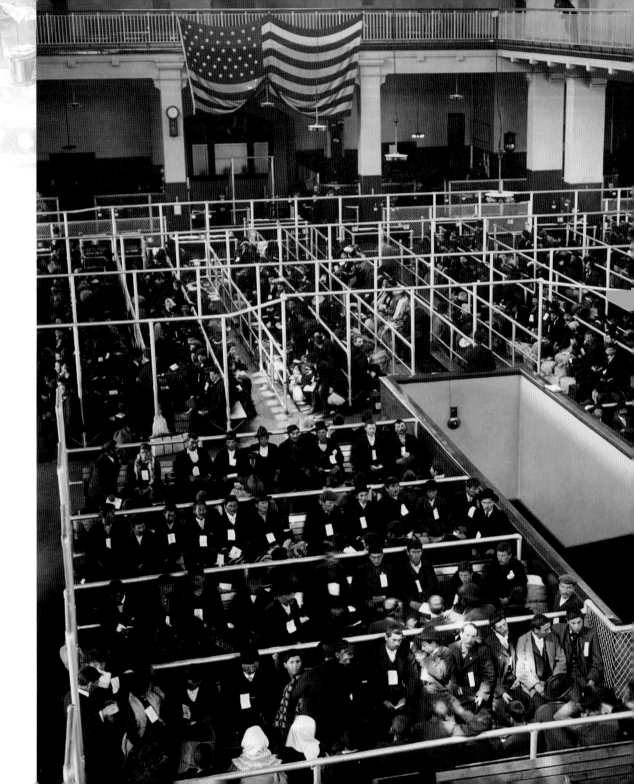

US cities quickly grew as more immigrants arrived at Ellis Island in New York throughout the late 1800s and early 1900s.

CHAPTER TWO

Big Business Pioneers

Toward the end of the 1800s, the United States entered a time of great change. The nation was becoming increasingly urbanized, especially in the Northeast. The Industrial Revolution, which began in the United Kingdom in the late 1700s and spread to the rest of Europe, had made its way to the Americas. The United States was slowly transforming from an agricultural nation into the leading manufacturing country in the world.

With the rise of industry and commerce came the rapid expansion of cities. Beginning in the 1850s, hundreds of thousands of people migrated from small towns and villages to work in the crowded metropolises. Immigrants traveled from countries such as Russia, Greece, and Ireland to start new businesses and establish new homes. Between 1870 and 1900, the population of US cities increased at triple the rate of rural areas. By 1900,

40 percent of Americans lived in cities. New York was the second-largest city in the world, with 3.5 million residents in all its boroughs combined.[1]

Before long, dozens of new companies cropped up around the country. Corporations such as US Steel and Ford Motor Company supplied tens of thousands of jobs to unskilled laborers willing to work long hours constructing much-needed resources such as steering wheels and brakes for automobiles. Men flocked to factories, eager to bring home enough money to support their families.

But men were not the only ones with jobs. By the time the 1900s had gotten under way, 19 percent of women had joined the workforce too.[2] In 1900, married mothers with children at home rarely held down jobs. But in contrast, almost half of single women were employed. Nearly 50 percent of those were involved in farming or hired on as domestic servants. And 25 percent more picked up jobs in textile mills and shoe factories.[3] It would be many decades before women could even contemplate obtaining jobs similar to

THE STRAW HAT PATENT

Betsey Metcalf designed the first straw hat in the United States. But she was afraid to register for a patent for the hats because all of the government licenses doled out at the time were reserved for products invented by men. In 1809, a woman named Mary Kies decided to challenge that long held tradition. She became the first woman to apply for a patent and, in doing so, took credit for Metcalf's creation. When Kies received the patent for the straw hat on May 15, 1809, First Lady Dolley Madison wrote a letter to thank Kies for her contribution.

those of men, let alone in leadership roles. But there were a few early pioneers who defied the odds and set the stage for businesswomen of the future.

Beauty Trailblazers

Most women who were employed outside the home during the 1900s spent their days doing what was considered women's work. They served as secretaries and bookkeepers for male-run businesses. Some worked as low-wage clerks selling clothes and beauty products for new retail giants such as Macy's and Nordstrom. Aside from the more skilled workers who landed jobs as teachers and nurses, the majority of women could be employed only in support staff positions.

But in 1905, an African-American laundress named Sarah Breedlove, who later changed her name to Madam C. J. Walker, set women on a path to change. After seeking treatment for a rare condition that made her hair fall out and receiving poor medical advice from her doctors, Walker developed her own remedy that combined the application of creams with the use of heated combs. Unlike most beauty products available at the time, which were geared toward white women, Walker's products were marketed specifically to African Americans.

Walker revolutionized the beauty industry by tapping an underdeveloped market. By selling her hair tonics door to door and interacting directly with her clients, she gained a loyal following of repeat customers and got ideas for new innovative products. As money began to pour in, she opened training schools in Denver, Colorado; Pittsburgh, Pennsylvania; and Indianapolis, Indiana, to provide women with much-needed jobs and teach them her skills. Walker hired more than 3,000 of

Walker called her
hair system the
Walker Method.

the women she trained to work in her factories and act as her sales force.[4] When she had extra money, she funded educational scholarships for women and donated large sums of money to dozens of black charities. By the time of her death at age 51 in 1919, the Madam C. J. Walker Manufacturing Company was worth more than $1 million.[5] Walker was one of the first US women to become a self-made millionaire—a remarkable accomplishment during a time when African Americans were still considered inferior to whites.

Not long after Walker's company started turning a profit, another woman was busy making waves in cosmetics: Canadian Elizabeth Arden, born Florence Nightingale Graham. Arden studied to become a nurse. Though she did not practice medicine for long, she picked up a few tricks that proved useful later, such as using creams to treat burn victims. When she moved to New York City in 1908, the first job she could find was in a salon. Arden enjoyed the work so much that in 1910,

COSMETIC RIVALRY

Elizabeth Arden was one of the most popular names in cosmetics during the early 1900s. But another woman was competing for the spotlight and was often referred to as Arden's rival: Helena Rubinstein. Born in Krakow, Poland, in 1872, Rubinstein started out in Australia selling her mother's favorite skin ointments made from herbs, almonds, and fir tree extract. The creams became so popular with Australian locals that Rubinstein opened a beauty shop in Melbourne in 1903. Working long hours and enlisting the help of a family friend and chemist to create more skin products, she expanded her business abroad by opening more salons in the wealthiest sections of London, England, and Paris, France, in 1908, and in New York in 1915. There, women could not only get pampered, but also learn how to use makeup and color to express their personalities. Rubinstein was also the first to invent waterproof mascara in 1938.

Arden's US beauty company became one
of the first global brands.

she opened a spa of her own on Manhattan's ritzy Fifth Avenue.

In the early 1900s, makeup was worn mostly by lower-class women. But Arden aimed to change that assumption by marketing the idea that women of every class could look beautiful and respectable by using lipstick and mascara to accentuate their natural features. She hired a team of chemists to develop a line of high-end skin care products that might appeal to her customers. Then she offered in-store makeovers to attract new clients who might walk in off the street. Finally, she sold travel-sized items and ointments for busy women on the go.

Arden's business model was a huge hit in New York and soon spread to other cities throughout the United States. In the 1920s, she opened salons in France and in countries across Europe and South America. By the 1930s, Arden's company was often referred to as one of the three best-known US brands in the world alongside Coca-Cola and Singer Sewing Machines. In 1946, Arden was the first woman to grace the cover of *TIME* magazine. By the time of her death in 1966, at the age of 81, Arden had opened more than 100 stores worldwide.[6] In 2015, her company was worth $999.3 million.[7]

REVOLUTIONIZING BEAUTY ONE FRAGRANCE AT A TIME

French fashion designer Gabrielle "Coco" Chanel was equally well known during the 1940s. Though Chanel enjoyed a brief career as a nightclub singer, she opened her first store selling hats in Paris in 1913. As business expanded, she sold clothes she designed herself.

In 1922, business skyrocketed when Chanel introduced the world to what would become her iconic perfume: Chanel No° 5, the first fragrance to be named after its designer. Building on its success, she launched many more trendsetting fashion campaigns throughout her career, including the chic and versatile little black dress and the timeless Chanel suit, which featured a collarless jacket and well-fitted skirt. When Chanel died in 1971 at the age of 87, many of the mourners who attended her funeral wore Chanel suits in her honor.

Women Flood the Labor Force

As World War I (1914–1918) raged overseas and men were drafted or volunteered to fight, thousands of jobs were left empty. Women entered the workforce in record numbers to take their places. Some women worked in plants that manufactured weapons and machine parts. Others worked on assembly lines, making much-needed munitions and resources for the war effort.

A member of the International Ladies' Garment Workers' Union fixes a blouse in a dress shop.

Companies became so desperate to meet the growing demand for supplies that women's employment rose 35 percent in rubber and photographic supplies, 33 percent in leather items, and 27 percent in electrical products. By the end of 1918, women made up 20 percent of the workforce in all manufacturing industries in the United States.[8]

Alongside the increase of women in the workforce came the rise of labor unions that fought for and protected the rights of their members. An early example was the International Ladies' Garment Workers' Union, which formed in 1900. New networking organizations provided education, mentorship, and support for female entrepreneurs hoping to start their own businesses. One of the first was the National Federation of Business and

Professional Women's Clubs, founded in 1919.

Female-focused employment agencies started cropping up around this time too. Carrie Crawford Smith was an African-American woman born in Tennessee in 1877. After attending Fisk University there, she moved northward to a Chicago suburb in search of work. Sensing a lack of opportunity for women of her race, she started one of the first recruiting companies geared toward African-American women in 1918. She helped hundreds of women find jobs as domestic help in Chicago and the surrounding area.

As men began trickling home from the war in 1919 and resumed their former positions, the number of jobs for women declined. But the entrepreneurial spirit that drove women to work during the war years did not dissipate. In the decades to come, women would forge new pathways in business, tackling a wide variety of professions in finance, cooking, engineering, and more.

SMITH'S STANDARDS

Carrie Crawford Smith's employment agency was groundbreaking for many reasons. For one, it found housekeeping jobs for the thousands of unemployed African-American women migrating north from the South during and after World War I. It also changed the way these housekeepers were treated on the job.

The Smith Employment Agency Standards and Principles stated that potential employers could not degrade African-American women in their work environments. Smith felt that crawling around on one's hands and knees—even while cleaning—was demeaning. No matter how much her rules displeased her white customers, Smith would not back down in enforcing them, even if it meant losing money. For her, preserving her maids' dignity was more important than revenue.

A group of women march in a parade for women's rights in New York City in 1912.

CHAPTER THREE

Empowered by the Vote

I n the decade following World War I, the United States entered a time of great prosperity. As the economy transitioned from wartime to peacetime production, opportunities in business and manufacturing exploded. The increasing availability of the automobile signaled a more convenient form of travel. New technologies such as home refrigeration, the automatic dishwasher, the electric air conditioner, and the pop-up toaster made housework and cooking easier. Between 1920 and 1929, the nation's wealth more than doubled.

On top of an expanding consumer culture, the world was changing drastically in other ways—especially for women. The Nineteenth Amendment to the US Constitution, passed by Congress on June 4, 1919, and ratified on August 18, 1920, guaranteed women the right to vote. Later that same year, more than eight million women across the country voted in elections for the first time.[1]

On the job front, women were more involved than ever. At the start of the 1920s, women represented 21 percent of the labor force—a jump up from 19 percent two decades earlier.[2] They worked in agriculture, manufacturing, domestic, and clerical positions. More married women were finding work outside the home too. A US census survey taken in January 1920 showed that of the more than eight million women who were employed, 23 percent were married—an increase of nearly 5 percent since 1890.[3] On June 5, 1920, the Women's Bureau of the Department of Labor was established to help women find jobs and protect their rights while employed. It was a good time for women in the working world.

Banking Icons

With the United States' booming economy and the increase of women in the workforce came the need for financial assistance and regulation. New banks appeared around the country to help people manage their money and provide loans to business owners. Most of these financial institutions were run and staffed by well-educated men.

But one bank was unique—as were its trailblazing founders. In 1922, two sisters, Clara and Lillian Westropp, opened the Women's Savings & Loan Company in Cleveland, Ohio. Directed and run solely by women, it was the first bank of its kind in the nation to address the economic needs of women. It served male clients, but it also sought to empower women by providing them with financial advice and the tools they needed to manage their savings and investments on their own—resources they did not have access to in the past.

In addition to helping women locally, the Westropps' bank grew to be successful nationwide. After earning a federal charter in 1935, which established it as a national corporation, the bank reorganized under the name Women's Federal Savings & Loan. Nearly 20 years later, it was the third-largest savings and loan institution in Ohio's Cuyahoga County. By 1983, when the company reorganized again and was renamed Women's Federal Savings Bank, it had more than $576 million in assets.[4]

HELPING WOMEN HELP THEMSELVES

Sisters Clara and Lillian Westropp helped thousands of women take control of their finances during the 1920s and beyond. In 1952, the Cuyahoga Savings & Loan League chose Clara as its president, the first woman to serve in that position. After she died in 1965, she was awarded the Mission Secretarial Award from Washington, DC, making her Catholic Woman of the Year. A lawyer and judge by trade, Lillian was one of the first women admitted to the Cleveland Bar Association and the first woman elected to the organization's executive committee. She served as president of the Women's Federal Savings & Loan Association from 1936 to 1957 and as chairman of its board of directors until her death in 1968.

Families were forced to wait in lines for food during the Great Depression.

Success Despite the Great Depression

The 1920s, full of art, culture, and extravagance, was a time of great freedom and wealth for many Americans. But by the end of 1929, most had suffered a disastrous financial setback. When the stock market crashed in October, the fallout triggered a global economic depression. Investors lost billions of dollars, sending the industrial world and families everywhere into a panic.

This was the start of the Great Depression. It was the longest-lasting economic downturn the world had experienced up to that point. Food and gas supplies were scarce. Unemployment levels soared. But despite the grim state of affairs, two women created new businesses that would thrive over time.

Margaret Rudkin and her family lived in Connecticut on a large estate. In 1937, at the age of 40, she baked her first loaf of bread. Her homemade recipe soon sparked a nationwide craving. Rudkin first sold a few loaves to local grocers. Within a year, she was baking 4,000 loaves

THE FIRST LADY OF AVIATION

During the Great Depression, Olive Ann Mellor Beech's family experienced a financial setback. But the young girl with a knack for numbers excelled in business even as a kid. She had a bank account by the time she was seven and later managed her family's finances. After marrying Walter Beech in 1930, the couple founded the aviation company Beech Aircraft in 1932. Beech took over the business when Walter died in 1950. Sales tripled during her years as president. The company supplied aircraft to NASA's *Apollo* and space shuttle programs.

Beech was the first woman to receive the National Aeronautic Association's Wright Brothers Memorial Trophy. In 1943, the *New York Times* named her one of 12 most distinguished women in the United States. And in 1970, *Fortune* magazine called her one of the ten highest-ranking women executives in major US corporations.[5]

Rudkin started baking bread as a way to
make ends meet after the stock market
crash of 1929.

each week for a specialty food store in
New York City.[6] By 1940, Rudkin had moved
her company, Pepperidge Farm, to an old
factory in Norwalk, Connecticut. In 1947, she
opened the first Pepperidge Farm bakery
in Norwalk.

Rudkin's bakeries produced 50,000
loaves per week, plus new types of sweets
including coffee cake and goldfish crackers.[7]
To keep up with the demand, Rudkin
continued to be on-site daily to make sure
everything was being done properly. At
the time of Rudkin's death in 1967, her
now world-famous company was selling
70 million loaves annually.[8]

Meanwhile, an African-American woman
from Louisiana named Hattie Moseley Austin
was busy perfecting her fried chicken recipe.
Despite the racial prejudice and enforced
segregation in 1938, Austin took her life

savings of $33 and opened Hattie's Chicken Shack in Saratoga Springs, New York.[9]

When the tiny eatery opened near the famous Saratoga racetrack, many prejudiced neighbors refused to enter. But before long, Austin's cooking earned a reputation with blacks and whites alike. For the next 40 years, people continued to flock to her place to grab a plate of Louisiana-style grub. By the time Austin, then in her mid-90s, sold the restaurant to new owners in 1993, her business was known throughout the country.

As the 1930s came to a close, the United States was on the upswing after a decade-long recession. The number of jobs had rebounded. In the two decades to come, women in the workplace would fill the vacancies in factories left by men shipped overseas to fight in World War II (1939–1945). Others would start businesses creating products for a new type of woman: the suburban housewife.

CONNECTICUT WOMEN'S HALL OF FAME

Much of Pepperidge Farm's success was due to Rudkin's talent for business. She was one of the first businesswomen to use television ads to promote her products. When she sold Pepperidge Farm to Campbell Soup Company in 1961, she became the first woman to serve on its board of directors. After her death in 1967, Rudkin was inducted into the Connecticut Women's Hall of Fame in 1994. In 2007, *Fortune* magazine's 100 Years of Power named her the most powerful woman in business for 1950–1960.

Women again took over many jobs while men were overseas fighting World War II.

CHAPTER FOUR

The Domestic Era

Between 1939 and 1945, World War II devastated countries across the globe. Tens of thousands of US servicemen and servicewomen journeyed overseas, mostly to Europe and Asia. Back on the home front, war-oriented production boomed. Unemployment virtually disappeared.

An increased need for skilled labor opened up new opportunities for women. They took jobs as welders, electricians, and riveters, manufacturing defense materials such as bomber planes. By the time the war was over, the percentage of women in the US workforce had grown from 27 percent to nearly 37 percent.[1]

Within a year of the war ending, jobs became much less available for women. Male soldiers returning home replaced many female workers. Companies that continued to hire women put them in entry-level positions and paid them lower wages. Over the next five years, women scrambled to

The iconic image of a bandana-wearing factory worker showing her arm muscle was the showpiece of a government campaign aimed at convincing women to work in munitions factories during World War II. The image was known as Rosie the Riveter. To this day, it is still considered one of the most successful recruitment efforts in history and an enduring symbol of female empowerment. The portrait was partly based on a real factory worker named Rosie Will Monroe, who fled her impoverished rural Kentucky background to find work in a city. She got a job at the Willow Run factory in Michigan, which trained female pilots to fly airplane parts around the country. Because she was a single mother, Monroe was not chosen for the flight program. But she made a career out of assembling planes in order to support her family.

look for ways to make up for their loss of revenue. A sharp increase in companies founded or run by women began. The Federation of Business and Professional Women's Clubs held educational workshops for budding entrepreneurs. From 1945 to 1950, the number of female-owned businesses jumped from 600,000 to nearly one million.[2]

Flaunting Style

After the war, when wartime rationing of food and supplies had subsided, the United States saw a return to consumer spending and a wealthier middle class. It was the perfect environment for a savvy businesswoman like Dorothy Shaver to take the shopping experience to a new level. Born in Center Point, Arkansas, in 1893, Shaver moved with her sister to New York City in 1916. The girls started a business crafting rag dolls, which were stocked by the upscale department store Lord & Taylor. The dolls were a hit, landing Shaver an entry-level job at the multimillion-dollar department store in 1921.

Many of the new businesses in the later
1940s involved female-centric products
such as makeup and fashion.

Shaver pioneered the concept of the branch store by expanding into the suburbs.

Over the next 20 years at Lord & Taylor, Shaver learned how to compete in the fashion business and was promoted to increasingly important management roles. Along the way, she made a number of influential changes and boosted the company's sales. She launched a series of successful marketing campaigns promoting the idea that women could be casual but flawlessly elegant by wearing Lord & Taylor clothing. Shaver offered new personalized services to shoppers looking for advice, attracting thousands of new customers who returned to the store often because of its exemplary customer service. In 1945, she became the first female president of Lord & Taylor and was offered $110,000—the equivalent of a man's salary.[3] The following year, the Associated Press named her "the outstanding woman in business."[4]

Women loved the new American look Shaver showcased inside Lord & Taylor stores and in their gorgeous window displays. Devoted shoppers championed the idea that a woman's beauty should be both accentuated and admired. By wearing expertly tailored clothing, a lady could project an image of grace and confidence under any circumstances.

STYLE AT *SEVENTEEN*

In the 1940s, Estelle Rubinstein set her sights on making a difference for teenagers in the fashion and cosmetics worlds. In 1944, a newly conceived *Seventeen* made a name for itself as the first magazine targeting teenage girls. Rubinstein, then 25, was its promotion director. Her first advertising campaign featured a 16-year-old girl named Teena. Teena was 5-foot-4 (163 cm), weighed 118 pounds (54 kg), and hoped to go to college, get married, and raise children. Rubinstein's ads attracted scores of investors. By the end of its first year, the magazine had also acquired more than one million readers, thanks in part to the appeal of Rubinstein's Teena.[6]

In addition to flaunting a stylish wardrobe, women in the 1940s and 1950s also thought it was important to camouflage aging—and no other beauty aids worked better at that time than Estée Lauder's. Inspired by Arden's success two decades earlier, Lauder launched her own cosmetics company in 1946. Two years later, Lauder acquired her own beauty counter at Saks Fifth Avenue. There, she pioneered the innovative free-gift-with-purchase concept that many modern cosmetics companies still use today.

Over the course of the next 60 years, Lauder transformed a one-woman shop into a global corporation by convincing generations of women that "the pursuit of beauty is honorable."[5] In 1960,

Lauder starting off selling
face lotions and makeup to
high-end salons and hotels.

she nabbed her first international account at Harrods department store in London and took her business overseas. At the time of her death in 2004, at the age of 97, the Estée Lauder Company had an estimated worth of $10 billion and staffed more than 21,500 employees. To this day, Lauder's products are sold in more than 130 countries.[7]

Domestic Goodies

As the 1940s came to a close, the tide of women heading into the labor force ebbed, dropping to 30 percent of all workers.[8] Most women who had jobs were employed in clerical positions or in professional jobs such as nurses or librarians. But the trend of female-owned and run businesses showed no sign of slowing down.

While more and more families moved from the bustling urban areas into the spacious planned communities of the suburbs, a new crop of female business owners began peddling their wares to the masses. And this time, they had a new focus:

BETTE NESMITH GRAHAM MAKES NO MISTAKE

Many of the products women championed during the 1950s were geared toward the home. But Bette Nesmith Graham made history when she invented a groundbreaking product for the office in 1954. At the time, most secretaries typed letters and documents using manual or electric typewriters that required paper and ink. When they made mistakes, they often had to rip out the paper and start over. Graham made the whole process more efficient. She created a white correction liquid for painting over typing errors and called it Mistake Out. By 1958, she was selling 100 bottles a month to other secretaries. In 1968, when she went on the road to sell more, the number was up to 40,000 bottles a week. In 1977, Graham's firm boasted 331 employees worldwide and sold a whopping 500 bottles each minute.[9] Before the advent of the computer, Graham's Mistake Out was one of the most commonly used items in US offices.

the domestic housewife who took care of the kids while her money-making husband commuted to work in the city. In 1950, Brownie Wise, a woman with only an eighth-grade education, started planning Tupperware parties to make additional money. She sold the new kitchen products to homemakers during invitation-only gatherings in their living rooms. The sales approach was so successful that Earl Tupper, the plastic storage products' inventor, appointed her the vice president of his company. Wise is widely credited with earning the company millions and being the reason for Tupperware's long-lasting success. She also earned a reputation for being the type of boss who recognized women who received little recognition elsewhere in their lives. During her tenure at the company, Wise gave her employees trophies, promotions, and plenty of praise for a job well done.

In 1951, 24-year-old German immigrant and mom-to-be Lillian Vernon made shopping easier for busy moms on the go who did not have time to hunt for bargains amidst their domestic responsibilities. She launched one of the first mail-order businesses, a company that sold clothing and household products through catalogs and shipped them via the postal service. Vernon sold purses, combs, cuff links, and belts. By 1982, she had totaled more than $62 million in sales and expanded her

Vernon stands with some
of the items available
through her catalogs.

Handler's company Mattel continues to create Barbie dolls with new interests and looks.

product line to include holiday decor and knickknacks for the home.[10]

Perhaps one of the most successful businesswomen in the United States in the 1950s was Ruth Handler. Born to Polish Jewish immigrants in 1916, Handler grew up with little money. She married her high school sweetheart and moved to Hollywood when she was 19. In 1945, the two founded a toy company called Mattel. The company soon became profitable, and Handler started contributing her own ideas for toys geared more toward girls. In 1959, she came up with a product design that would soon make history: a plastic doll with long flowing hair, blue eyes, and a perfectly trim figure. She named the doll Barbie after her daughter, Barbara.

Handler's invention was important for many reasons. For one, it was one of the first toys geared not toward younger children, as was popular at the time, but toward teenage girls with defined tastes and career aspirations. More important, the doll's evolving wardrobe reflected the changing values in US culture. During the civil rights movement in the 1960s, Mattel produced Barbie's first black friend, Francie. In the 1970s, during the women's equal rights movement, Barbie's outfits reflected new job interests. She became a doctor, a veterinarian, and an astronaut, inspiring young girls nationwide to reach for the top in their careers.

"My whole philosophy of Barbie was that through the doll, the little girl could be anything she wanted to be," Handler wrote in her 1994 memoir, *Dream Doll: The Ruth Handler Story*. "Barbie always represented the fact that a woman has choices."[11]

More Freedom to Come

The carefully managed life in the suburbs was ideal for many Americans during the 1950s because it provided a break from the bustling pace of the cities and gave millions of kids a safe haven in which to grow into adolescents. But by the end of the decade, some stay-at-home moms and housewives began to grow restless. Many wanted more than a life of cooking and cleaning.

Throughout the 1960s and 1970s, a number of positive changes would take place. The second wave of feminism and the fight for equal rights not just for women, but for minorities as well, would emerge. A new age for women in business was fast approaching.

Eleanor Roosevelt, *left*, and John Kennedy meet before the start of the Commission on the Status of Women.

CHAPTER FIVE

Feminists and Civil Rights

The 1960s and 1970s were a tumultuous period in the United States. The country faced many problems including the ongoing Vietnam War (1955–1975), the Cold War (1947–1991), and a widening divide between economic classes. Two of the most controversial issues were civil rights for minorities and equal freedom and representation for women.

In 1960, there were approximately 25 million women working outside the home, accounting for 37 percent of the total workforce. But women earned an average of 59 cents on the dollar compared with men.[1] Women of all races were becoming frustrated with being treated as less than equal. In 1961, President John F. Kennedy established a Commission on the Status of Women, with former First Lady Eleanor Roosevelt as its first chairperson. The goal of the committee was to study how women were treated on the job.

The results, released in a report in 1963, were not surprising. Women, especially minorities, were not treated as equals in the US workplace. They

Jean Nidetch

(1923–2015)

I n the 1960s and 1970s, women were as concerned with their appearances as in previous decades. Stylish shoes and flawless makeup were crucial—and so was being able to fit into a favorite pair of jeans. Jean Nidetch helped weight-conscious women everywhere look their best by providing them with a surefire method to stay in shape and look great.

In 1961, the 214-pound (97 kg) New York housewife with a weakness for sweets ran into a friend at the grocery store. Mistaking Nidetch's weight problem for a pregnancy, the friend asked Nidetch when the baby was due. Nidetch was mortified. Over the next two years, she went on a diet, exercised, and lost 72 pounds (33 kg). Along with her overweight husband and two friends, she then formed Weight Watchers in 1963.

For Nidetch and millions of women, Weight Watchers became the key to losing weight—and keeping it off. The program featured weekly meetings; weigh-ins and food diaries; and a lean, nutritional diet devoid of alcohol, fattening foods, and sweets. By 1968, five million people around the world had enrolled.[2]

were passed over for jobs. Those who did manage to get hired received lower salaries than their male counterparts. Title VII of the Civil Rights Act of 1964 aimed to prohibit this type of employment discrimination on the basis of race, religion, national origin, and gender. But the wage and opportunity gap persisted. Outraged women began banding together as part of a nationwide movement calling for women's liberation at home, in society, and in the workplace.

Symbols of Achievement

Despite the unequal playing field of the 1960s and 1970s, more women were taking chances and rising to the top at work than in the past. Following in the footsteps of the pioneering entrepreneurial women who came before them, others started their own companies.

Rose Morgan was already one of the most successful African-American businesswomen of her generation. During a time when most spas and salons catered to wealthy white clientele, she opened a barbershop in New York in 1942 geared toward lower- and middle-class minorities. Thanks in part to its affordable prices and its popular services such as braids and weaves, it became the largest African-American beauty parlor in the country within four years.

Morgan aimed her sights even higher in the 1960s. She wrote a column for the *New Pittsburgh Courier* called The Beautiful Truth: Rose Morgan's Beauty Tips. The ongoing articles provided advice to thousands of women of color overlooked by fashion magazines targeting white readers. In 1965, Morgan was the first African-American beauty shop owner to become a member of the New York State Wage Board, a group in charge of reviewing salaries and conditions for workers within the state.

Roddick was a passionate activist for
many different causes, which was
reflected in her business model.

She also helped found New York's only black-owned commercial bank, the Freedom National Bank.

During the 1970s, other women made their mark on the beauty industry as well. In 1976, then-British housewife Anita Roddick was taking care of her two daughters while her husband was fulfilling his dream of riding from Buenos Aires, Argentina, to New York on a horse. To keep herself busy in his absence, she opened a beauty-supply store in Brighton, England, called The Body Shop.

At first, The Body Shop sold the usual fare: skin creams, hair products, and some makeup. But having spent most of her adolescence and early adulthood traveling to far-flung countries and learning the traditions of other cultures, Roddick wanted to expand her business beyond one store into a franchise that was socially, environmentally, and ethically responsible. Instead of shelving products tested on animals, Roddick sold only those that were cruelty-free and made from organic or non-harmful ingredients. All of the paper and plastic containers used in the store were made from recycled materials.

By the time of her death in 2007, Roddick had opened more than 2,000 stores that served upwards of 77 million customers worldwide.[3] The respect she garnered was not just because she was one of the world's most successful female entrepreneurs. Roddick used her influence and vast fortune to promote and fund worthwhile causes. In 1990, she established Children on the Edge, a charity for children in Europe and Asia. That same year, she helped found the *Big Issue*, a magazine written and produced by homeless people. In 2001, she partnered with Greenpeace and other environmental organizations to wage an international campaign against Exxon-Mobil, the world's largest oil and gas conglomerate, to bring attention to the company's antienvironmental practices.

"Anita did more than run a successful ethical business: she was a pioneer of the whole concept of ethical and green consumerism," Tony Juniper, director of Friends of the Earth, wrote in the *Evening Standard*. "There are quite a few business

MRS. FIELDS COOKIES

When 20-year-old housewife Debbi Fields opened her cookie store in Palo Alto, California, on August 16, 1977, she did not have any business experience. But she made a bet with her husband that she could sell at least $50 worth of cookies the first day. By enticing potential customers on the street with free samples, she beat her estimate by $25. Since then, the Mrs. Fields cookie franchise has expanded into a $450 million dessert empire, with 700 stores in ten countries.[4] Fields's secret to success is to never lose the excitement she felt on her first day. She wants every customer to have a good experience.

people today who claim green credentials, but none came anywhere near Anita in terms of commitment and credibility."[5]

New Fields of Opportunity

In 1970, more and more women like Morgan and Roddick were taking charge of their destinies and forming companies that could give back to the world. But they needed access to something very important: money. Beginning in the mid-1970s, a change was taking place in the financial industry. In the past, large loans were usually made available only to men. Banks considered women to be poor credit risks. But as more and more women were becoming business owners, a rising need for easily accessible cash began to surface. To answer the demand, new female-friendly credit unions and banks began to pop up, starting with the Feminist Federal Credit Union in Detroit, Michigan, in 1973 and the First Women's Bank in New York in 1975. Now women could finally take advantage of some of the same opportunities as their male counterparts.

The change helped. Between 1972 and 1979, the number of self-employed women increased from 1.5 million to 2.1 million.[6] In addition to becoming independent business owners, more women were making great strides in the corporate world too. They were branching out into fields that were previously considered men's work.

Single mother Marsha Serlin started the first female-owned recycling company in 1978 with $200 and a rental truck. At first, no one took her seriously, because she was a woman in a

AN INVENTOR OVERSEAS

In the 1970s, women in other countries were accomplishing groundbreaking feats in other countries. In India, Kiran Mazumdar-Shaw started her career as the country's first female master brewer. But after failing to find a job in the field, the then 25-year-old built on her knowledge of mixing industrial enzymes and started her own biotech company out of her garage in 1978. At first, because she was a woman, investors would not take her seriously. But still she persevered. In 2013, her company employed more than 6,000 people. One year later, it had $460 billion in revenue and was selling its products in 85 countries.[9] It is now widely considered to be one of India's premier biopharmaceutical companies.

male-dominated field. So she held down other jobs to make ends meet and pay the bills. She sold insurance at night, ran the counter at her brother's clothing store on the weekends, and picked up scrap metal during the weekdays. The first few years were tough. But by 2012, United Scrap Metal employed 200 people and was worth more than $200 million.[7] "I was the first woman to do this . . . I think the thought was, 'She'll be gone in three months, in six months,'" Serlin told the *Chicago Tribune* in 2012. But she proved her detractors wrong. "As long as [competitors] were forecasting that I would fail, I could focus on my operation. They had no respect for women. Most of the companies who gave me a rough time, they're gone. And I'm here."[8]

Perhaps the most promising development was in the male-centric field of technology—a ripple that set the course for the rest of the 1900s. In the early 1970s, Sandra Kurtzig was employed as a salesperson for General Electric when a client came to her with an important dilemma. He was frustrated by his company's inability to keep track of its inventory. Always up for a challenge and searching for a way to be able to work from home after she had children, Kurtzig used her undergraduate math degree to write a computer software program that could manage inventory and maintain production schedules.

After the project was finished, Kurtzig used the idea to form her own business. Working out of her spare bedroom in 1974 with $2,000 in her pocket, she founded ASK Computer Systems—the first female-owned and run computer company. Prospective clients were leery at first. But Kurtzig used her gender—and her sense of humor—to her advantage. She created flyers with headlines that read, "Warning: Dangerous Woman on the Loose."[10]

Within just a few years, ASK was one of the fastest-growing computer software companies in the United States. In 1981, Kurtzig became the first woman to take a technology firm public. By 1992, her fledgling operation had blossomed into a company worth $450 million. And throughout the next two decades, Kurtzig would continue to serve as a role model for generations of women forging new paths in technology and beyond.

Laws
Helping Women

During the 1960s and 1970s, three laws helped women achieve greater equality in the workplace and in all aspects of life. They earned the right to work and to choose when to start a family.

- Signed into law by President John F. Kennedy on June 10, 1963, the Equal Pay Act of 1963 was one of the first federal antidiscrimination laws that addressed wage differences based on gender. After it passed, the practice of paying men and women different salaries for the same work at the same job became illegal.

On July 2, 1964, President Lyndon B. Johnson signed into law the Civil Rights Act of 1964. The legislation outlawed discrimination on the basis of race, color, religion, national origin, or gender. It required equal access to public places and employment and enforced desegregation of schools.

The Equal Credit Opportunity Act of 1974, signed by Gerald R. Ford, made it illegal for creditors to discriminate against applicants based on race, color, religion, national origin, marital status, age, or sex. Equal access to credit changed women's abilities to open their own businesses.

Susan Hager, *left*, meets with President Jimmy Carter, *center*, and other business leaders at the White House in 1977.

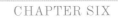

CHAPTER SIX

Franchising Women

T he 1980s was an important decade for women in business. The hard work of feminists during the previous generations was beginning to pay off. According to the US Bureau of Labor Statistics, 51.5 percent of women worked in 1980, as compared with 77.4 percent of men.[1] Female entrepreneurs owned 25 percent of all companies in the United States.[2]

Slowly, Americans were growing more comfortable with the idea that a woman could do as good a job at work as a man. A new crop of business networking organizations started materializing around this time to spread the word. Founded by Susan Hager in 1975 in Washington, DC, the National Association of Women Business Owners (NAWBO) was one of the first organizations to offer financial strategy classes and business-growth seminars to women interested in starting their own firms.

"Through NAWBO, women business owners were able to meet and turn to one another for support and information," Hager said.[3]

NAWBO did not just help women in Washington. In fact, there were so many young businesswomen interested in learning the ropes that 21 satellite chapters were established in 30 states across the country and in 17 countries abroad by the mid-1980s.[4]

Hoping to mirror NAWBO's mission and success, the Women's Business Development Center opened its doors in Chicago in 1986. It held workshops and conferences about topics such as financing, marketing, and business development. Three years later, NAWBO launched a separate arm of its organization dedicated to researching and publishing articles, periodicals, and books about women's leadership in business. Called the Center for Women's Business Research, the offshoot was instrumental in keeping all areas of society informed about the female entrepreneurs' movement.

BORN TO LEAD

Susan Hager was the oldest of seven children in her family. Her leadership skills at home proved to be beneficial for her career. In 1973, she and her business partner, Marcia Sharp, founded Hager Sharp Inc., a public relations firm. The company began with one client.

"[Hager] wanted to control her destiny and be her own boss at a time when it was not easy for women to do so," Hager's daughter, Elizabeth Finley, told the *Washington Post*. "She wanted to make it better for herself and other women."[5]

Like many female entrepreneurs at the time, Hager had a hard time securing a loan from a bank to fund her start-up. So she used her experience to start NAWBO in 1975. Today NAWBO has more than 8,000 members in 80 chapters across the country.[6]

Businesswomen as Brands

It was in this environment of learning and sharing information that the idea that a female business owner could start out in one field and expand into another was born. Already a stockbroker on Wall Street by the time she was 25, Martha Stewart moved to Westport, Connecticut, in 1972 and started a small catering company four years later. In the 1980s, her career really took off.

With the publication of her first book, *Entertaining*, in 1982 and the slew of others that followed, Stewart became the go-to source for guides to flawless etiquette and stylish living. But she did not stop there. She became a brand. Over the next two decades, her company Martha Stewart Living Omnimedia launched two magazines—*Martha Stewart Living* and *Martha Stewart Weddings*—which between

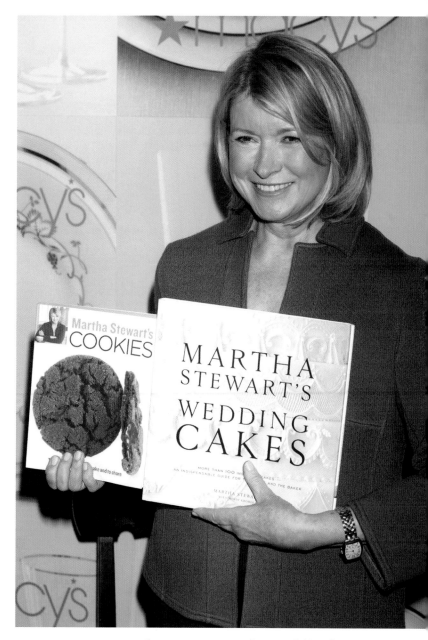

Stewart wrote several successful books on cooking, baking, and lifestyle tips.

them reached ten million readers. Stewart also started a weekday radio show, which aired on 270 stations, and an Ask Martha column that ran simultaneously in 233 newspapers. Two television shows and the sale of thousands of merchandized products followed.[7]

Another high-powered multimedia businesswoman who set the cultural pulse for the 1980s and beyond was Oprah Winfrey. With her daytime program *The Oprah Winfrey Show* beginning in 1986, Winfrey transformed the gossip-heavy talk show format into a place where women could discuss their feelings, find inspiration, and learn how to thrive in their daily lives. By its last taping in 2011, *The Oprah Winfrey Show* attracted 48 million weekly viewers in the United States and more than 150 countries.[8]

Jumping on her show's Number 1–rated success, Winfrey pioneered other trends over the next 30 years. She started the magazine *O*; her own production company, Harpo Productions; and cable station the Oprah Winfrey Network (OWN)—the first network named for, and inspired by, a single iconic leader. Her book club inspired millions of people worldwide to read and sparked $55 million in

THE DOWNSIDE OF SUCCESS

At the height of Stewart's success in 1999, her empire was worth $2 billion.[10] But when Martha Stewart Living Omnimedia was sold on June 22, 2015, it went for a fraction of what it was once worth. Perhaps the biggest reason for Stewart's downfall was the five-month prison term she served in 2004 after being convicted of insider trading, an illegal practice of using confidential or dishonestly obtained information to buy or sell stocks. As a result, her television show was canceled. She resigned from Martha Stewart Living Omnimedia's board of directors. Stewart was ordered to pay back $195,000 in related charges.

sales of the more than 70 books she featured on her show.[9] In 2015, she nabbed the fifth slot on *Forbes* magazine's prestigious America's Richest Self-Made Women list, with a net worth of $3 billion.[11] Winfrey is slated to launch a new publishing imprint of nonfiction titles about famous inspirational people, including her memoir, in 2017. "All of my experiences, even the painful ones, have been there to teach me something about life," Winfrey said in her memoir's press release. "I'm still learning and I hope my story inspires other people to live the highest, fullest expression of themselves."[12]

A Nation of Immigrants

The 1980s was a decade full of golden business opportunities for women such as Stewart and Winfrey. But these prospects were not limited to women born in the

Winfrey started as a successful talk show host before branching out to other ventures.

United States. More immigrants were finding success too. Thai Lee was born in Bangkok, Thailand, but raised in South Korea. She came to the United States for college and then attended Harvard Business School. In 1989, Lee and her husband bought a failing information technology provider and formed SHI International, with Lee as the company's CEO. Today, SHI International has $6 billion in sales from more than 17,500 customers. It is the largest female-owned business and one of the largest minority-owned companies in the United States.[13]

After moving to the United States from South Korea in 1981, Jin Sook Chang and her husband took a chance. In 1984, they opened a small clothing store in Los Angeles, California, called Fashion 21. With the $700,000 they made in earnings the first year, the couple opened a new store every six months. Today their chain is called Forever 21. In 2015, Forever 21's earnings amounted to approximately $4.4 billion. Chang, the franchise's chief merchandising officer, was the United States' fourth-richest self-made woman in 2015, according to *Forbes*.[14] "Forever 21 gives hope and inspiration to people

Forever 21 consists of more than 700 stores worldwide.

who come [to the United States] with almost nothing," said Chang's husband, Do Won, in an interview with the *Los Angeles Times*. "And that is a reward that humbles me: the fact that immigrants coming to America, much like I did, can come into a Forever 21 and know that all of this was started by [Korean immigrants] with a dream."[16]

Lee and Chang arrived in the United States during the 1980s with little more than a vision for a prosperous future. With hard work and dedication, they succeeded. In the decades to come, others would continue to follow in their footsteps. In the United States, becoming an influential businesswoman was no longer a far-off dream accessible by only a few. It was becoming a commonplace reality.

It became more common to see
women in executive positions
in the 1990s.

CHAPTER SEVEN

Working Women Count!

As the United States entered the last decade of the 1900s, women made up nearly half of the labor force. Nearly 58 million women in total were employed. They worked for pay in greater numbers, for more years, and in more occupations. According to the US Women's Bureau's estimate in 1994, 99 percent of women in the United States would work for pay at some point in their lives.[1]

During the 1990s, work shifted from the industrial economy to the knowledge economy. Manufacturing and factory jobs decreased as more human workers were replaced by computerized machines. Increasing reliance on the Internet meant more people had access to tech-related jobs than they had in the past. Women started receiving more degrees in the hopes of starting their own companies. By 1989, women received nearly half the undergraduate degrees awarded in business nationally and almost one-third of all advanced degrees in business administration.[2]

Female entrepreneurs were also facing new challenges. A 1994 survey conducted by the US Women's Bureau found the two top-ranking priorities for working women in the 1990s were improving pay scales and health-care insurance. As more mothers held down day jobs, the problem of juggling time at the office with a fulfilling life at home had also come to the forefront:

> The number one issue women want to bring to [President Bill Clinton's] attention is the difficulty of balancing work and family obligations. They report that problems with child care are deep and pervasive, affecting families across the economic spectrum.[3]

But the fight for reform was in full swing. And, as always, a number of dynamic and talented women were leading the charge.

THE PINNACLE OF SUCCESS

Nina Vaca was born in Ecuador and moved to the United States with her parents when she was two years old. Being an immigrant can be a difficult experience for many. Because Vaca's parents were both entrepreneurs, the family worked hard to get by. Then tragedy struck. Vaca's father was killed in a robbery when she was still in high school, leaving her and her sister in charge of his travel agency. They sold the business after a year, and in 1996, 25-year-old Vaca used the skills her parents had taught her and $300 she had in savings to start an information technology service provider called Pinnacle Technical Resources. The company's first few years were difficult. It almost folded many times. But in 2011, Pinnacle became the largest female-owned and Hispanic-owned vendor management software firm in the world. In 2015, Vaca's company was worth $650 million.[4]

Movers and Shapers

Television buffs probably associate actress Sofía Vergara with her role in ABC's Emmy Award–winning sitcom *Modern Family*, which aired its first episode in 2009 and averaged 12 million viewers an episode in its third season. The program's success, combined with Vergara's endorsement deals and

Vergara is not only a beautiful actress, but also a smart businesswoman.

sales from her Kmart fashion line, earned her the title of 2012's "highest paid TV actress" at $19 million.[5] But what many fans might not know is that she is also a savvy businesswoman.

In 1995, Vergara traveled to the United States from her native Colombia to host a travel show for the Univision Network. Within a year, she and business partner Luis Balaguer cofounded a small Miami-based talent scouting firm for Hispanic actors called Latin World Entertainment (LWE). This was a demographic without any substantial representation at the time. The move proved to be a wise one. Over the course of 20 years, LWE blossomed into a licensing, marketing, and production phenomenon, with clients such as Disney and Paramount Pictures. Its annual revenue reached $27 million.[6] "The truth is out that [Latinos] are in this country and we're taking over," Vergara told *Forbes* in 2012. "To see people paying attention to the cultural changes that Luis and I have seen coming for a long time is fantastic."[7]

Sara Blakely was another shrewd businesswoman who shaped the course of the 1990s—literally. In 1998, at the age of 29, Blakely emptied her savings account of $5,000 and set out to create a product that could help women look slim no matter what they were wearing. Her family assured Blakely that the shaping underwear she called Spanx would be the perfect gift for friends and friends of friends. But six months later, the onetime door-to-door fax machine salesperson and Disney World ride greeter was shocked to find out the product was a hit with Winfrey—and the media mogul's worldwide audience.

"My dad encouraged us to fail. Growing up, he would ask us what we failed at that week. If we didn't have something, he would be disappointed. It changed my mindset at an early age that failure is not the outcome, failure is not trying. Don't be afraid to fail."[8]

—*Sara Blakely*

Over the next decade and a half, Blakely expanded her company to attract even more consumers. She added shaping yoga apparel, bodysuits, jeans, and even snug undergarments for men. In 2015, she made Number 17 on the

Forbes America's Richest Self-Made Women list, earning $1.09 billion. Blakely was the first female billionaire to sign on for the Giving Pledge, Bill Gates and Warren Buffett's pledge to entice the world's richest people to give at least half of their wealth to charity.[9]

Learning Curves

Perhaps the most radical change in business toward the end of the 1900s happened because of advances in technology. Once hugely expensive, the personal computer had become more affordable for the average person. By the late 1990s, the World Wide Web was more commonplace, and sending letters by e-mail was becoming more commonplace. It was clear people searching for new jobs and higher positions were looking for networking resources that could help them succeed.

Blakely shows off her Spanx at the 2012 *TIME* 100 gala.

An amateur entrepreneur named Laurel Touby had an idea for a business that would provide those tools. In 1994, Touby was an overworked, underpaid freelance writer living in New York City. She was tired of attending and often hosting the endless parade of meet-and-greet events that did not seem to get her anywhere. So in 1996, she launched a website called Mediabistro.com. It featured job listings and, later, career development courses, articles covering media-industry-related news, and even health insurance options for freelancers.

Word of Touby's website spread, and within just a few years, it was the Number 1 social networking site for people working in publishing and the arts. Touby sold the company in 2007 for $23 million.[10] In 2013, the website had an international base of more than two million members.[11] "Way before anyone else, she saw there was a market for niche online classifieds," said Cyndi Stivers, founding editor of *Time Out New York*. "On a certain level, she did it instinctively. She also had a really good eye for talent."[12]

BUSINESS 2.0

In 1982, Lynda Weinman's boyfriend at the time asked her to help him with his new computer. After teaching him some of the basics, she realized she had a knack for explaining technical information in simple terms. Eleven years later, when she was teaching at Art Center College of Design in Pasadena, California, she bought the Lynda.com domain name for $35. Then she wrote a book about how to use the then-new World Wide Web and uploaded educational how-to videos online. The book became an international best seller. Weinman sold Lynda.com to LinkedIn for $1.5 billion in April 2015—the fourth-largest deal in social media history.[13]

Touby's simple and innovative website idea
made her millions of dollars.

Mediabistro.com made Touby rich and affirmed her reputation as a smart leader. It also
symbolized the dawn of a new age. In the new millennium, female entrepreneurs and those just
starting out would have more access to knowledge and each other than ever before. Though unequal
pay and workplace discrimination would remain serious issues in the 2000s, opportunities for new
businesses—and women's roles in them—seemed endless.

The number of minority-owned businesses quickly grew in the 2000s.

CHAPTER EIGHT

Business in the New Millennium

The outlook for women in business in the United States during the 2000s had completely transformed since the early 1900s when women did not have the right to vote. More women in the 2000s were starting their own businesses than ever before. Between 1997 and 2007, the number of female-owned businesses increased by 44 percent, from 5.4 million to 7.8 million.[1]

Businesses started by women of color were finally becoming more commonplace as well. According to the US Department of Commerce, Economics and Statistics Administration, between 1997 and 2002, the number of minority female-owned businesses increased at a faster rate than those owned by white women. Out of all ethnic and racial groups, the rate of African-American female-owned companies grew the most, gaining more than 234,000 businesses during the five-year time period—an increase of 75 percent. In 2002, Hispanic women owned slightly more than 34 percent of minority businesses.[2]

The US government did its part to foster this growth. In 2000, Congress mandated that female small business owners should receive 5 percent of federal contracts each year.[3] Despite the seemingly low number, this allowed women more access to business opportunities and federal funding than they had in the past. "Federal government contracts are an enormous opportunity for women to help increase their revenues by billions each year," said Barbara Kasoff, president and chief executive of the organization Women Impacting Public Policy, in an interview with the *New York Times*.[4]

A SOLE-FUL COMPANY

Bethlehem Tilahun Alemu used natural resources to engineer a truly innovative product. In the early 2000s, in a small village near the Ethiopian capital of Addis Ababa, Alemu and her neighbors were struggling to make ends meet. But in 2004, she came up with a solution that would solve their financial woes and fill a need. She founded soleRebels, a company that makes sandals, flip-flops, and boots out of recycled tires and locally grown koba plants, organic cotton, and jute. The company is now one of Africa's fastest growing and most popular footwear brands. The company projects opening 50 soleRebels retail stores across the United States by 2018 and 500 worldwide by 2022. In 2011, *Forbes* named Alemu one of the 20 Youngest Power Women in Africa.[5]

Global Ventures

Thanks in part to the increase in government money and the availability of loans from private investors, female entrepreneurs in the early 2000s had access to more of the tools they needed to operate on a global scale. Because of the world's increased

Kasoff is a firm believer
in women taking charge
in the business world.

dependence on the Internet by the year 2000, many business ventures could now reach a worldwide audience.

Following in Madam C. J. Walker's footsteps, Chaundra Smith founded the beauty company Naturally Me in 2008. Instead of relying on in-person sales, Smith quickly reached a wider audience by marketing to spas and boutiques and featuring a full array of natural products made without animal-derived ingredients on her company's website. "My biggest challenges at this point are expanding my reach to a broader target audience, as well as converting social media followers into customers," Smith said. "I am now blogging more and sponsoring more events."[6]

Other businesswomen capitalized on the growing influence of social media and the existence of information-sharing websites. In the late 1990s, Caterina Fake was one of the first online graphic designers and bloggers during a time when posting personal content was just beginning. During the 2000s, she founded a trio of websites: the photo-sharing service Flickr, which was acquired by Yahoo in 2005 for $35 million; the decision-making website Hunch, which was acquired by eBay in 2011 for $80 million; and Findery, an app for discovering art and notable historic destinations in nearly every country in the world.[7]

A New Trend: The Female CEO

The first ten years of the 2000s were a boon for female business owners. But in addition to founding their own companies, women were also getting treated with more respect in the

corporate workplace. A few were even being hired as presidents, chief executive officers (CEOs), or chief operating officers (COOs) of multibillion-dollar firms.

Businesswoman and 2016 presidential candidate Carly Fiorina is a true female CEO pioneer. When she was hired to be the technology company Hewlett-Packard's CEO in 1999, she became the first woman to take control of a Fortune 100 company. But her rise to power and fortune did not happen overnight.

After obtaining a liberal arts degree from Stanford University, Fiorina attended the University of California, Los Angeles law school and promptly dropped out after her first year. When she told her father what she had done, he voiced his disappointment and told her she would not get very far. But Fiorina proved him wrong. After working as a secretary and teaching English in Italy, she got a job at telecommunications company AT&T when she was 25. From there, she earned an advanced degree in business from the University of Maryland while keeping her job at AT&T. At age 40, despite being surround by mostly men in AT&T's Network Systems division, she was appointed head of North American sales.

After a strong start, Fiorina
dropped out of the presidential
race in February 2016.

Marissa Mayer

(1975–)

Born on May 30, 1975, Marissa Mayer grew up in the small town of Wausau, Wisconsin. The daughter of an engineer and an art teacher, Mayer excelled in math and science at school. Though she applied to Stanford University intending to become a doctor, she switched majors to earn an undergraduate degree in science. Soon after, she received an advanced degree in computer science, with a specialization in artificial intelligence.

In 1999, Mayer took a job with Google. At the time, the Internet search engine had only 19 employees. She became its twentieth and Google's first female engineer. After more than a decade at Google working on programs such as Gmail and Google Maps, the then-underperforming search engine Yahoo recruited Mayer. In 2012, she was appointed Yahoo's president and CEO and joined the ranks of female CEOs such as Fiorina. In September 2013, *Fortune* ranked Mayer Number 1 in its annual 40 Under 40 list of business leaders.[9]

In 1998, *Fortune* named Fiorina the most powerful woman in business. The following year, Hewlett-Packard was so impressed by Fiorina's leadership skills and top-notch track record that it appointed her CEO of the company. There, Fiorina not only streamlined business operations but also launched the Technology for Teaching program to help bring technology to underserved communities around the world.

Perhaps the most well-known COO is Sheryl Sandberg. After working as a Google executive for nearly seven years starting in 2001, the Harvard Business School graduate took a job with Facebook as its COO in 2008 and became the first woman on the social networking website's board. In 2013, she published the best-selling *Lean In: Women, Work, and the Will to Lead*, a book that uses case studies to highlight gender inequality in the United States, and offers practical advice to help women take charge of their lives and become more proactive and confident in their careers. A year later, she offered tailored advice to college students in *Lean In for Graduates*. In 2015, Sandberg was ranked the eighth most powerful woman in the world, according to *Forbes*, with a net worth of $1.3 billion.[10]

Fiorina and Sandberg are just two examples of businesswomen who have shaped social, economic, and technological progress during the 2000s. By consistently demonstrating that women as leaders can be just as competent as men, they have proven themselves equal partners in a world where communication and cooperation between sexes is a must. But the fight for gender equality is not over. As Sandberg says, "No industry or country can reach its full potential until women reach their full potential."[11]

Anne-Marie Slaughter's work away from her home and family was taking a toll, which sparked an important choice for Slaughter.

CHAPTER NINE

Looking Ahead

I n 2010, 18 months into a two-year stint as the first female director of policy planning at the US State Department, Anne-Marie Slaughter faced an important choice. As a lifelong advocate for women's equality in business, she had worked hard to get where she was and loved her job. But her home life was suffering. She saw her husband and two young boys only on weekends. They lived in Princeton, New Jersey, while Slaughter worked three hours away by car in Washington, DC.

"I was increasingly aware that the feminist beliefs on which I had built my entire career were shifting under my feet. I had always assumed that if I could get a foreign-policy job in the State Department or the White House while my party was in power, I would stay the course as long as I had the opportunity to do work I loved," Slaughter said in the *Atlantic*.[1]

Slaughter left the world of government. She returned to New Jersey to teach and be with her family. One year later, she published a seminal article in the *Atlantic* entitled "Why Women Still Can't Have It All." In it, she debunked commonly held half-truths including "It's possible if you are just

committed enough" and "It's possible if you marry the right person."[2] Slaughter presented a sobering picture of why so many US women found it difficult to succeed in today's fiercely competitive business environment. The sad truth is that for Slaughter and so many other women juggling long hours at the office and at home, creating a work-life balance can often seem nearly impossible.

The Good, Bad, and Ugly

In 2014, women made up 50.8 percent of the US population. According to the Center for American Progress (CAP), they earned nearly 60 percent of undergraduate degrees and 60 percent of all master's degrees. More than 44 percent of advanced degrees in business and management were awarded to women. They represented 47 percent of the US labor force and held almost 52 percent of all professional-level jobs.[3]

The last decades of the 1900s saw considerable progress in women's career advancement in the United States. Sex discrimination in most workplaces ebbed. And more women landed management jobs. That is the good news.

But despite the fact that women have come a long way since the 1900s, they are still underrepresented in leadership positions. According to 2014 figures from CAP, women represent only 14.6 percent of CEOs and 8.1 percent of top earners. Women of color occupy 11.9 percent of managerial and professional positions.[4] CAP estimates as late as 2012, women still only made eighty-one cents at the most for every dollar a man earned, depending on their ethnicity.

Female Leaders:
By the Numbers

These days, women hold more leadership positions in business than ever before. But we still have a long way to go before the playing field is equal. Here is a breakdown of women in management in the 2000s, organized by industry.[5]

- Women make up 54.2 percent of the financial services workforce, but only 12.4 percent are executive officers and 18.3 percent are board directors. None are CEOs.

- Women make up 78.4 percent of the health-care and social services workforce, but only 14.6 percent are executive officers and 12.4 percent are board directors. None are CEOs.

- Women make up 34.3 percent of all physicians and surgeons but only 15.9 percent are medical school deans.

- Women make up 9 percent of management positions in the tech industry, and only 14 percent have senior management positions at tech start-ups.

- Women make up 4.6 percent of Fortune 500 CEOs, but women of color hold only 3.2 percent of the board seats, and more than two-thirds of Fortune 500 companies have no women of color on their boards at all.

Ingrid Vanderveldt

(1970–)

Ingrid Vanderveldt has worn many hats over the course of her decades-long career. For many years she was a host on television's CNBC news channel. In 2011, she acted as the tech company Dell's first Entrepreneur in Residence, where she launched a website populated with inspirational interviews and useful information to help global entrepreneurs navigate the stages of business ownership. She also went on the road and interviewed thousands of women about their career goals and needs.

In addition to working inside companies, Vanderveldt also started a few of her own. She served as the CEO of Green Girl Energy, the first energy company developed by and for women. Today, as the founder and chairwoman of EBW2020 and MintHER, she is on a mission to empower a billion women by 2020 by giving them the technology, education, and networking opportunities they need to become successful leaders. "I fundamentally believe that if we are going to create the change we want to see in the world, we must view sustainability through the eyes of women," Vanderveldt said.[6]

That is $897 per week on average for a white man, $734 for a white woman, $611 for an African-American woman, $841 for an Asian-American woman, and $548 for a Hispanic or Latin-American woman.[7]

As Slaughter points out in her *Atlantic* article, the potential path of a modern businesswoman—especially those who are also mothers—is not the same as it is for a modern businessman. Men and women are still treated unequally. Yet even in the face of the glaring discrepancies in pay and perception, a slew of female innovators are making their mark on the 2000s.

A Smorgasbord of Start-ups

At 31, Elizabeth Holmes is the world's youngest self-made female billionaire, according to *Forbes*. In 2015, President Obama named her a US ambassador for global entrepreneurship. She became the youngest person ever to be awarded the Horatio Alger Award in recognition of "remarkable achievements accomplished through honesty, hard work, self-reliance and perseverance over adversity." *TIME* pegged her as one of the 100 Most Influential People in the World.[8] She is also on the Board of Fellows of Harvard Medical School.

A MIGHTY ACCOMPLISHMENT

On November 18, 2015, Elizabeth Holmes was rated Number 6 on *Forbes*'s America's Richest Entrepreneurs Under 40 list. The title is a huge accomplishment for the 31-year-old, who experienced difficulties finding investors for Theranos not just because she was so young, but also because she was a woman in a field dominated by men who didn't take her seriously. But the list itself is not such a bonus for women on the whole. Out of the 40 people named, the other 39 were all men.

Holmes's rise to fame began when she dropped out of Stanford University at 19 years old. Rather than finish her education, she founded Theranos, a company working to develop a new, cheaper finger-prick technology that would bypass the reliance on needles in blood testing for diseases. During her start-up's first few years, Holmes made every part of her life about work. Throughout her 20s, she worked seven days a week.

Holmes is still Theranos's CEO. Since its beginnings in 2003, the company has raised more than $400 million. It is now valued at $9 billion.[9] Though Theranos was accused of cheating in 2015 by supposedly using other companies' technologies to analyze many of the tests it was conducting for consumers, Holmes insists these accusations were false and is determined to restore her company's integrity. "What we need to do now is focus on the technology and focus on the science and the data and put that out there," she told *Bloomberg* magazine. "Because that speaks for itself."[10]

FROM GOOGLE MAPS TO FASHION

In 2008, former Hong Kong native and Stanford University graduate Jess Lee was a product manager for Google Maps. In her spare time, she browsed Polyvore, a search engine site for fashion and shopping. Then, after a chance meeting with the founders of the site, Lee was offered a job as their product manager. She accepted. In 2007, she was made an official cofounder of the company and soon jumped to CEO. Under her direction, Polyvore blossomed into the largest fashion site on the Internet, with 20 million users by 2012. In 2015, Yahoo acquired it for $230 million.[11]

Other women are focusing their efforts on the fun side of life, inventing products and online sites to make Americans' daily routines easier. In 2012, Kellee Khalil founded Lover.ly, a visual search engine and cloud-based scrapbook for everything wedding-related. The site's content is tagged for color, season, location, and clothing brand to make it easily accessible for potential brides-to-be. In her first year of business, Khalil raised $1 million in her race to become the top website for wedding planning.[12]

Tracy Sun spent two years working as the vice president of merchandising and inventory planning at the female-founded clothing store Brooklyn Industries. But in 2010, she decided to create her own venture. After teaming up with cofounders Manish Chandra and Chetan Pungaliya, the trio launched Poshmark, a website and app that lets consumers browse, buy, and sell clothing and accessories from other people's closets. Already hugely successful with more than one million members, the shopping destination is a cross between Pinterest and eBay for women's clothes.

Alexa Andrzejewski used her obsession with food to start her own business. Once a user experience designer at Adaptive Path, she left the design and consulting firm in 2010 to cofound Foodspotting. This crowdsourcing app allows users to upload and tag food-related photos from their travels. The site became so popular that OpenTable purchased it in 2013 for $10 million.[13]

Looking to the Future

From medicine to shopping to technology to food, women are inventing fresh ways to do business in all areas of US culture and throughout the world. Thanks to new financing opportunities and

Khalil attends a Martha Stewart Weddings
party in 2015.

technologies that make business ownership more manageable, more women are heading start-ups than ever before. And the potential for groundbreaking opportunities seems endless.

Still, as Slaughter reminds us, there is more work to be done. Women are not yet equal to men in leadership representation or pay. Businesswomen of color have even larger hurdles to overcome. But the push for gender equality is far from fading.

Throughout the 1900s and into the 2000s, women's individual efforts combined to deliver a unified message in the world of entrepreneurship: We embrace the power of possibility. We have the will and passion to transform lives. And most important, we are here to stay.

"All my life, I'd been on the other side of this exchange. . . . I'd been the woman congratulating herself on her unswerving commitment to the feminist cause . . . I'd been the one telling young women at my lectures that you can have it all and do it all, regardless of what field you are in. Which means I'd been part, albeit unwittingly, of making millions of women feel that they are to blame if they cannot manage to rise up the ladder as fast as men and also have a family and an active home life (and be thin and beautiful to boot)."[14]

—Anne-Marie Slaughter (the Atlantic, July/August 2012)

Timeline

1905

Madam C. J. Walker founds her own line of beauty products and later becomes one of the first female self-made millionaires.

1910

Elizabeth Arden opens her first salon in New York City.

1920

The Women's Bureau of the Department of Labor is founded on June 5; the Nineteenth Amendment is ratified on August 18.

1922

Clara and Lillian Westropp open the Women's Savings & Loan Company in Cleveland, Ohio—the first bank directed and run by women.

1945

Women compose nearly 37 percent of the workforce in the United States; Dorothy Shaver becomes the first female president of Lord & Taylor.

1959

Ruth Handler, coowner of Mattel, designs the first Barbie doll.

1963

The Equal Pay Act of 1963 is passed on June 10 and is one of the first federal antidiscrimination laws that addresses wage differences based on gender.

1974

Sandra Kurtzig founds ASK Computer Systems later becoming the first women to take a technology firm public in 1981.

1978

Marsha Serlin starts the first female-owned recycling company, which is worth $200 million 34 years later; Kiran Mazumdar-Shaw founds Biocon, now India's largest publicly traded biopharmaceutical company.

1986

The Oprah Winfrey Show airs its first episode, launching Oprah Winfrey into a star-studded career.

1989

Thai Lee cofounds SHI International, the largest female-owned business and one of the largest minority-owned in the United States.

1990

Women make up nearly half of the labor force—nearly 58 million workers in total.

1999

Carly Fiorina is hired to be Hewlett-Packard's CEO, becoming the first woman to take control of a Fortune 100 company.

2007

The number of female-owned businesses reaches 7.8 million.

2011

Kimberly Bryant founds Black Girls CODE.

2013

Facebook COO Sheryl Sandberg publishes *Lean In: Women, Work, and the Will to Lead*, a best seller that sparks a nationwide movement arguing for women's equality in the workplace.

2014

Women are 47 percent of the US labor force and hold almost 52 percent of all professional-level jobs.

2015

President Obama names Elizabeth Holmes, founder of Theranos, a US ambassador for global entrepreneurship; Yahoo buys Polyvore for $230 million.

Essential Facts

KEY PLAYERS

- Anita Roddick, a bath and cosmetics company owner who used The Body Shop to advance philanthropic agendas such as global warming and recycling

- Carly Fiorina, Hewlett-Packard's CEO and the first woman to take control of a Fortune 100 company

- Kimberly Bryant, founder of Black Girls CODE, an organization that teaches girls computer programming skills

- Madam C. J. Walker, one of the United States' first female millionaires and creator of beauty products for African-American women

- Oprah Winfrey, publisher, writer, actress, talk show host, philanthropist, and spiritual guide for millions of Americans

- Sheryl Sandberg, Facebook COO and author of *Lean In: Women, Work, and the Will to Lead*

- Sofía Vergara, actress and cofounder of Latin World Entertainment, the premier talent agency for Latin American entertainers

WOMEN IN THE BUSINESS WORLD

Women have made great strides in business over the last 100 years. Until the early 1900s, married women with children rarely worked outside the home. Most working women were single and worked as domestic servants or in factories, especially during World War I and II as men were shipped overseas to fight. In the 1960s and 1970s as women began to strive for equal rights and access to loans became more available, they began opening their own businesses. In the 1980s, women advanced in entertainment and media. During the 1990s, they gained leadership positions in technology. By the turn of the 2000s and into the 2010s, as the Internet grew, business opportunities for women are more possible than ever before. Today, most women do not earn as much as men. Juggling motherhood and daily employment is still a struggle. But women are one step closer to achieving true equality in business.

IMPACT ON SOCIETY

Throughout the 1900s, women fought for their inalienable rights during times when they were seen as unequal to men. In the 1920s, women won the right to vote. In the 1960s, they earned the right to work and to choose when to have children. And in the 1980s, a percentage of government funding was set aside for women hoping to start their own companies. Through all of these milestones, businesswomen of all races and colors were key in facilitating change. Though they continue to be paid less than their male counterparts and are often passed over for leadership positions because of their gender, female entrepreneurs' products and services continue to transform culture in the United States and around the world.

QUOTE

"Failure is not the outcome, failure is not trying. Don't be afraid to fail."
—*Sara Blakely*

Glossary

BIOTECH
A company that uses living organisms or other biological systems in the manufacture of drugs or other products.

BRAND
A name or mark a company uses to distinguish its products from those of other companies.

CROWDSOURCING
The process of obtaining needed ideas or content by soliciting contributions from a large group of people, and especially from an online community.

DESEGREGATION
The elimination of laws, customs, or practices under which people from different religions, ancestries, or ethnic groups are restricted to specific or separate public facilities, neighborhoods, schools, or organizations.

DISCRIMINATION
Unfair treatment of other people, usually because of race, age, or gender.

ENTREPRENEUR
A person who organizes and operates a business or businesses.

FEMINISM
The belief that women should have the same opportunities and rights as men politically, socially, and economically.

FRANCHISE
An authorization granted by a government or company to an individual or group enabling them to carry out specified commercial activities.

FREELANCE
Working for different companies at different times rather than being permanently employed by one company.

INDUSTRIAL REVOLUTION
The rapid development of industry that occurred in Britain in the late 1700s and 1800s and migrated to the United States, brought about by the introduction of machinery.

LABOR UNION
An organized association of workers, often in a trade or profession, formed to protect and further their rights and interests.

MOGUL
An important or powerful person.

NICHE
A place or activity for which a person or thing is best fitted.

PHILANTHROPY
The act of making charitable donations for the purpose of improving human welfare.

PRESTIGIOUS
Inspiring respect and admiration; having high status.

RATIFY
To formally approve or adopt an idea or document.

RECESSION
A period of negative economic growth and, usually, low demand for goods and high unemployment.

REVENUE
Income, especially of a company or organization and of a substantial nature.

SAVVY
Having practical knowledge or understanding of something.

SEGREGATION
The practice of separating groups of people based on race, gender, ethnicity, or other factors.

SHREWD
Having or showing sharp powers of judgment.

VERSATILE
Able to adapt to many different functions or activities.

Additional Resources

SELECTED BIBLIOGRAPHY

"From Ideas to Independence: A Century of Entrepreneurial Women." *National Women's History Museum*. National Women's History Museum, n.d. Web. 22 Feb. 2016.

Inverso, Emily. "The World's Most Powerful Women Entrepreneurs of 2015." *Forbes*. Forbes, 26 May 2015. Web. 22 Feb. 2016.

Slaughter, Anne-Marie. "Why Women Still Can't Have It All." *Atlantic*. Atlantic Monthly Group, July/Aug. 2012. Web. 22 Feb. 2016.

FURTHER READINGS

Anderson, Jennifer Joline. *Women's Rights Movement*. Minneapolis, MN: Abdo, 2014. Print.

Cornell, Kari A. *Women on the US Home Front*. Minneapolis, MN: Abdo, 2016. Print.

Lusted, Marcia Amidon. *The Fight for Women's Suffrage*. Minneapolis, MN: Abdo, 2012. Print.

WEBSITES

To learn more about Women's Lives in History, visit **booklinks.abdopublishing.com**. These links are routinely monitored and updated to provide the most current information available.

FOR MORE INFORMATION

For more information on this subject, contact or visit the following organizations:

Black Girls CODE
2323 Broadway
Oakland, CA 94612
510-398-0880
http://www.blackgirlscode.com
The Black Girls CODE website offers up-to-date information about local chapters and hackathons across the United States, as well as online resources for beginner and advanced computer programmers.

The National Women's Hall of Fame
76 Fall Street
Seneca Falls, NY 13148
315-568-8060
https://www.womenofthehall.org
The National Women's Hall of Fame is the country's oldest membership organization dedicated to honoring and celebrating the achievements of distinguished US women. The museum hosts interactive exhibits, lectures, and tours for visiting groups and schools.

Source Notes

CHAPTER 1. KIMBERLY BRYANT: CHAMPION OF CHANGE

1. "Oprah's The Life You Want Weekend." *Oprah*. Harpo Productions, 2015. Web. 2 Mar. 2016.

2. Laura Shumaker. "Oprah Gives San Francisco's Kimberly Bryant a Standing O-vation." *SF Gate*. Hearst, 17 Nov. 2014. Web. 2 Mar. 2016.

3. "Meet San Jose's Toyota Standing O-Vation Recipient." *Oprah*. Harpo Productions, 2015. Web. 2 Mar. 2016.

4. "Meet Miami's Toyota Standing O-Vation Recipient." *Oprah*. Harpo Productions, 2015. Web. 2 Mar. 2016.

5. "Meet San Jose's Toyota Standing O-Vation Recipient." *Oprah*. Harpo Productions, 2015. Web. 2 Mar. 2016.

6. Allie Bidwell. "Tech Companies Work to Combat Computer Science Education Gap." *US News & World Report*. US News & World Report, 27 Dec. 2013. Web. 2 Mar. 2016.

7. John Lauerman. "Nice Ivy League Degree. Now if You Want a Job, Go to Code School." *Bloomberg Business*. Bloomberg, 7 May 2015. Web. 2 Mar. 2016.

8. "Black Women in the United States, 2014." *Black Women's Roundtable*. National Coalition on Black Civic Participation, Mar. 2014. Web. 2 Mar. 2016.

9. Serena Williams. "The Ball Is in Your Court." *Wired*. Condé Nast, Nov. 2015. Web. 2 Mar. 2016.

10. Alexandra Phanor-Faury. "Black Girls Code's Kim Bryant Talks Bits and Bytes." *Ebony*. Ebony, 19 Mar. 2014. Web. 2 Mar. 2016.

11. "Margaret Fogarty Rudkin." *Encyclopedia.com*. Cengage Learning, 2004. Web. 2 Mar. 2016.

12. Serena Williams. "The Ball Is in Your Court." *Wired*. Condé Nast, Nov. 2015. Web. 2 Mar. 2016.

13. "Melinda Gates Biography." *Biography.com*. A&E Television Networks, n.d. Web. 2 Mar. 2016.

CHAPTER 2. BIG BUSINESS PIONEERS

1. William R. Merriam. *Census Reports: Volume I*. Washington, DC, 1901. *Google Book Search*. Web. 2 Mar. 2016.

2. Donald M Fisk. "American Labor in the 20th Century." *BLS.gov*. US Bureau of Labor Statistics, 30 Jan. 2003. Web. 2 Mar. 2016.

3. "Women's Occupations." *The First Measured Century*. PBS, n.d. Web. 2 Mar. 2016.

4. "Madam C. J. Walker Biography." *Biography.com*. A&E Television Networks, n.d. Web. 2 Mar. 2016.

5. Ibid.

6. "Elizabeth Arden Biography." *Biography.com*. A&E Television Networks, n.d. Web. 2 Mar. 2016.

7. "12 Female Entrepreneurs Who Changed the Way We Do Business." *CNN*. Cable News Network, 12 Apr. 2013. Web. 2 Mar. 2016.

8. "Employment of Women in War Production." *SSA.gov*. Bureau of Employment Security, n.d. Web. 2 Mar. 2016.

CHAPTER 3. EMPOWERED BY THE VOTE

1. "19th Amendment." *History*. A&E Networks, 2010. Web. 2 Mar. 2016.

2. Rebecca Onion. "Vintage Infographics: Where Women Worked in 1920." *Slate*. Slate Group, 11 Mar. 2013. Web. 2 Mar. 2016.

3. Ibid.

4. "Women's Federal Savings Bank." *Encyclopedia of Cleveland History*. Case Western Reserve University, 23 July 1997. Web. 2 Mar. 2016.

5. "Olive Ann Mellor Beech." *Kansapedia*. Kansas Historical Society, Jan. 2016. Web. 2 Mar. 2016.

6. "Margaret Fogarty Rudkin." *Encyclopedia.com*. Cengage Learning, 2004. Web. 2 Mar. 2016.

7. Ibid.

8. Ibid.

9. "75 Years of Hattie's." *Simply Saratoga*. Saratoga Publishing, 2015. Web. 2 Mar. 2016.

CHAPTER 4. THE DOMESTIC ERA

1. "Rosie the Riveter." *History*. A&E Networks, 2010. Web. 2 Mar. 2016.

2. "1940–1959 Postwar Pressures and Incentives: 1946-1950." *NWHM*. National Women's History Museum, n.d. Web. 2 Mar. 2016.

3. Ann T. Keene. "Dorothy Shaver." *American National Biography Online*. American Council of Learned Societies, 2000. Web. 2 Mar. 2016.

4. "Dorothy Shaver (1893–1959)." *National Museum of American History*. Smithsonian Institution, 2002. Web. 2 Mar. 2016.

5. Richard Severo. "Estée Lauder, Pursuer of Beauty and Cosmetics Titan, Dies at 97." *New York Times*. New York Times, 26 Apr. 2004. Web. 2 Mar. 2016.

6. Douglas Martin. "Estelle Ellis Rubinstein, a Pioneer at Seventeen, Dies at 92." *New York Times*. New York Times, 14 July 2012. Web. 2 Mar. 2016.

7. Richard Severo. "Estée Lauder, Pursuer of Beauty and Cosmetics Titan, Dies at 97." *New York Times*. New York Times, 26 Apr. 2004. Web. 2 Mar. 2016.

8. James P. Mitchell and Alice K. Leopold. "Changes of Women's Occupations: 1940–1950." *Women's Bureau*. United States Department of Labor, 1954. Web. 2 Mar. 2016.

9. "Bette Nesmith Graham." *NWHM*. National Women's History Museum, n.d. Web. 2 Mar. 2016.

10. "Lillian Vernon." *NWHM*. National Women's History Museum, n.d. Web. 2 Mar. 2016.

11. Sarah Kershaw. "Ruth Handler, Whose Barbie Gave Dolls Curves, Dies at 85." *New York Times*. New York Times, 29 Apr. 2002. Web. 2 Mar. 2016.

CHAPTER 5. FEMINISTS AND CIVIL RIGHTS

1. "Equal Pay Act of 1963." *National Park Service*. US Department of Interior, 22 Feb. 2016. Web. 2 Mar. 2016.

2. Robert D. McFadden. "Jean Nidetch, a Founder of Weight Watchers, Dies at 91." *New York Times*. New York Times, 29 Apr. 2015. Web. 2 Mar. 2016.

3. Anita Roddick. "About Dame Anita Roddick." *AnitaRoddick.com*. AnitaRoddick.com, n.d. Web. 2 Mar. 2016.

4. "More Than Cookies." *Debbi Fields*. Debbi Fields, n.d. Web. 2 Mar. 2016.

5. Sarah Lyall. "Anita Roddick, Body Shop Founder, Dies at 64." *New York Times*. New York Times, 12 Sept. 2007. Web. 2 Mar. 2016.

6. Patricia G. Greene, Myra M. Hart, Elizabeth J. Gatewood, Candida G. Brush, and Nancy M. Carter. *Women Entrepreneurs: Moving Front and Center: An Overview of Research and Theory*. University of New Mexico, n.d. Web. 2 Mar. 2016.

7. William Hageman. "Remarkable Woman: Marsha Serlin." *Chicago Tribune*. Tribune Company, 5 Aug. 2012. Web. 2 Mar. 2016.

8. Ibid.

9. "#85 Kiran Mazumdar-Shaw." *Forbes*. Forbes.com, 2016. Web. 2 Mar. 2016.

10. Lisen Stromberg. "Sandra Kurtzig: The Original Silicon Valley 'Mompreneur.'" *HuffPost Business*. TheHuffingtonPost.com, 8 July 2015. Web. 2 Mar. 2016.

Source Notes Continued

CHAPTER 6. FRANCHISING WOMEN

1. "Labor Force Participation Trends for Women and Men." *United States Department of Labor*. US Bureau of Labor Statistics, 18 Dec. 2001. Web. 2 Mar. 2016.

2. "1980s–1990s: Gaining Widespread Acceptance: The 1980s." *NWHM*. National Women's History Museum, n.d. Web. 2 Mar. 2016.

3. Yvonne Shinhoster Lamb. "Susan Hager, 63; Advocate for Female Business Owners." *Washington Post*. Washington Post, 4 Aug. 2008. Web. 2 Mar. 2016.

4. "40 Years of Impact." *National Association of Women Business Owners*. NAWBO, 2014. Web. 2 Mar. 2016.

5. Yvonne Shinhoster Lamb. "Susan Hager, 63; Advocate for Female Business Owners." *Washington Post*. Washington Post, 4 Aug. 2008. Web. 2 Mar. 2016.

6. Ibid.

7. Joan Didion. "Everywoman.com." *New Yorker*. Condé Nast, 21 Feb. 2000. Web. 2 Mar. 2016.

8. Murrey Jacobson. "The Oprah Effect, By the Numbers." *PBS NewsHour*. NewsHour, 25 May 2011. Web. 2 Mar. 2016.

9. Ibid.

10. Jacob Bogage. "How Martha Stewart Lost Her $2 Billion Empire." *Washington Post*. Washington Post 29 June 2015. Web. 2 Mar. 2016.

11. "#5 Oprah Winfrey." *Forbes*. Forbes.com, 2016. Web. 2 Mar. 2016.

12. Rachel Deahl. "Flatiron to Pub Oprah's Memoir, Host Her New Imprint." *Publishers Weekly*. PWxyz, 3 Dec. 2015. Web. 2 Mar. 2016.

13. "#14 Thai Lee." *Forbes*. Forbes.com, 2016. Web. 2 Mar. 2016.

14. "#4 Jin Sook Chang." *Forbes*. Forbes.com, 2016. Web. 2 Mar. 2016.

15. Colleen DeBaise. "25 Years Since Women Needed a Male Co-Signer." *Huffington Post*. TheHuffingtonPost.com, 25 Dec. 2013. Web. 2 Mar. 2016.

16. Ken Bensinger. "How I Made It—Do Won Chang." *Los Angeles Times*. Los Angeles Times, 31 Jul. 2010. Web. 2 Mar. 2016.

CHAPTER 7. WORKING WOMEN COUNT!

1. "Working Women Count!: A Report to the Nation." *Women's Bureau*. United States Department of Labor, 1994. Web. 2 Mar. 2016.

2. Tona Henderson. "Women in Business." *Reference for Business*. Advameg, 2016. Web. 2 Mar. 2016.

3. "Working Women Count!: A Report to the Nation." *Women's Bureau*. United States Department of Labor, 1994. Web. 2 Mar. 2016.

4. Octavio Blanco. "Nina Vaca: Daughter of Immigrants Now Runs a $650 Million Firm." *CNN Money*. Cable News Network, 29 Sept. 2015. Web. 2 Mar. 2016.

5. Meghan Casserly. "Sofia Vergara Tops the List of the Best Paid Actresses on Television." *Forbes*. Forbes.com, 18 July 2012. Web. 2 Mar. 2016.

6. Ibid.

7. Ibid.

8. "Sara Blakely." *NWHM*. National Women's History Museum, n.d. Web. 2 Mar. 2016.

9. "#17 Sara Blakely." *Forbes*. Forbes.com, 2016. Web. 2 Mar. 2016.

10. Penelope Green. "The Loft That Mediabistro Built." *New York Times*. New York Times, 14 Nov. 2012. Web. 2 Mar. 2016.

11. "Laurel Touby." *NWHM*. National Women's History Museum, n.d. Web. 2 Mar. 2016.

12. Penelope Green. "The Loft That Mediabistro Built." *New York Times*. New York Times, 14 Nov. 2012. Web. 2 Mar. 2016.

13. Emily Inverso. "Lynda Weinman Announces Exit as Executive Chair of Lynda.com." *Forbes*. Forbes.com, 10 June 2015. Web. 2 Mar. 2016.

CHAPTER 8. BUSINESS IN THE NEW MILLENNIUM

1. "Women-Owned Businesses in the 21st Century." *US Department of Commerce*. White House Council on Women and Girls, Oct. 2010. Web. 2 Mar. 2016.

2. Ibid.

3. Elizabeth Olson. "Women Business Owners Seek Better Access to Federal Contracts." *New York Times*. New York Times, 1 Oct. 2008. Web. 2 Mar. 2016.

4. Ibid.

5. Farai Gundan. "Fastest Growing African Shoe-Brand 'SoleRebels' Launches Flagship Store in Silicon Valley." *Forbes*. Forbes.com, 16 Oct. 2014. Web. 2 Mar. 2016.

6. "Chaundra Smith of Naturally Me: Treating Skin with Nature's Bounty." *Story Exchange*. Story Exchange, 4 Apr. 2014. Web. 2 Mar. 2016.

7. "Caterina Fake." *NWHM*. National Women's History Museum, n.d. Web. 2 Mar. 2016.

8. "Allison O'Kelly." *NWHM*. National Women's History Museum, n.d. Web. 2 Mar. 2016.

9. "Marissa Mayer Biography." *Biography.com*. A&E Television Networks, n.d. Web. 2 Mar. 2016.

10. "#1476 Sheryl Sandberg." *Forbes*. Forbes.com, 2016. Web. 2 Mar. 2016.

11. Susmita Baral. "International Women's Day Quotes: 37 Powerful Sayings about Gender Equality." *iDigitalTimes*. IBT Media, 7 Mar. 2015. Web. 2 Mar. 2016.

CHAPTER 9. LOOKING AHEAD

1. Anne-Marie Slaughter. "Why Women Still Can't Have It All." *Atlantic*. Atlantic Monthly Group, July/Aug. 2012. Web. 2 Mar. 2016.

2. Ibid.

3. Judith Warner. "Fact Sheet: The Women's Leadership Gap." *Center for American Progress*. Center for American Progress, 7 Mar. 2014. Web. 7 Dec. 2015.

4. Ibid.

5. Ibid.

6. Rieva Lesonsky. "Spotlight Interview: Ingrid Vanderveldt." *Dell*. Dell, 2016. Web. 2 Mar. 2016.

7. "Median Weekly Earnings by Sex, Race and Hispanic or Latino Ethnicity, 2014 Annual Averages." *US Department of Labor*. US Department of Labor, 2014. Web. 2 Mar. 2016.

8. James B. Stewart. "The Narrative Frays for Theranos and Elizabeth Holmes." *New York Times*. New York Times, 29 Oct. 2015. Web. 2 Mar. 2016.

9. Ibid.

10. Sheelah Kolhatkar and Caroline Chen. "Can Elizabeth Holmes Save Her Unicorn?" *Bloomberg Business*. Bloomberg, 10 Dec. 2015. Web. 2 Mar. 2016.

11. Leena Rao. "Polyvore's Jess Lee on Why She Sold to Yahoo." *Fortune*. Time, 16 Nov. 2015. Web. 2 Mar. 2016.

12. Lauren Drell. "44 Female Founders Every Entrepreneur Should Know." *Mashable*. Mashable, 6 Aug. 2012. Web. 2 Mar. 2016.

13. "Foodspotting." *CrunchBase*. CrunchBase, 2016. Web. 2 Mar. 2016.

14. Anne-Marie Slaughter. "Why Women Still Can't Have It All." *Atlantic*. Atlantic Monthly Group, July/Aug. 2012. Web. 2 Mar. 2016.

Index

About the Author

Alexis Burling has written dozens of articles and books for young readers on a variety of topics including current events, famous people, nutrition and fitness, careers and money management, relationships, and cooking. She is also a book critic with reviews of both adult and young adult books, author interviews, and other industry-related articles published in the *New York Times*, the *Washington Post*, *San Francisco Chronicle*, and more. Burling comes from a long line of women who started their own businesses. Her mother is a renowned fiber artist, and her great-grandmother opened and ran her own millinery shop full of gorgeous handmade hats.